Fly Fishing
for
SMALLMOUTH BASS

BY
JOE BRUCE

D1457611

K&D Limited, Inc.

Knowledge & Dedication

Published by
K&D Limited, Inc.
14834 Old Frederick Road
Woodbine, MD 21797
410-489-4967

Printed in the United States of America

ISBN 0-9637161-4-X

Library of Congress Cataloging-in-Publication Data

Bruce, Joe, 1946-
   Fly fishing for smallmouth bass : a mini-book / by Joe Bruce.
      p.   cm.
   ISBN 0-9637161-4-X
   1. Smallmouth bass fishing.   2. Fly Fishing.   I. Title.
   SH681.B85   1997
   799.1'77388--dc21   97-41329
                                                            CIP

Photos by author.
Cover and text design by Donna J. Dove, K&D Limited, Inc.

CONTENTS

I don't know how I would run the shop without Howard.

Hank at the counter, demonstrating the fine points of a reel.

4

Acknowledgements

All our lives we meet new people; some are just "passers by," some we get to know by face with no name attached, some have a name attached to that face, others are slight acquaintances, and some become friends. But occasionally, there are those special people that come into our lives by fate.

A truly special one is my shop assistant, Howard Wode. He's been my right-hand man for over six years. Without his hard work, patience and, yes, sometimes fatherly advice, this book could not have been written. The time and effort he's put into the shop has given me the freedom that I needed to go fishing and to gather the ideas and information to compile this book. I can't thank you enough, Howard!

Once again, I'm grateful for the assistance of my editor and friend, Hank Holland.

The father is Joe, the son is Rick — they're both older now, but still love fishing.

PREFACE

I am lucky enough to have grown up near some of the best smallmouth bass waters in the United States: the Shenandoah, Potomac and the Susquehanna Rivers. It was natural for my love of fishing to gravitate to these great rivers and their great fish. Smallies are by far the freshwater heavy-weights. They do all that you can ask of a fish, they slam the fly at times, they pull hard and they jump, and won't give up till they're in hand. What else can you ask for?

They are also found in the many streams and creeks off these rivers in settings that often will rival any picturesque trout stream.

This brings up the reason that this series of books was published in the first place. My goal is to introduce fly fishermen, whether beginners or advanced, to fishing opportunities beyond trout fishing. I have been fishing with a fly rod since I was sixteen years old, and have never lost my desire to fish for many different species. Although most people associate fly fishing with trout, the variety of fishing is boundless. Whether you enjoy fishing for panfish in ponds, bass in rivers, tarpon on the flats or shark in the ocean, they all can be successfully lured to a fly. Fly fishing has always been one of my greatest joys, next to my wife and family.

I have always been a strong believer that if you can teach or show someone how to do something, they will want to give it a try. Good information and help will accelerate learning by eliminating the pitfalls of teaching yourself, and will quicken the learning curve. These books reflect that belief.

As much as I love to fish, I take great pleasure in sharing my experience and accumulated knowledge with my fellow fly fishermen. At my fly shop, *The Fisherman's Edge* in Baltimore, Maryland, I try my best to educate our customers and help them understand the variety of techniques that can increase their success rate with the fly rod. With the kind of information presented here, I hope to make your fly fishing experiences happier and more fruitful, and shorten the learning process.

This book is part of a series of books on flies and fishing techniques for specific fish in certain types of water. The books are based on our experience not only in the Chesapeake Bay and surrounding area, but on many trips in various parts of the country. While they are intended to serve as a source of "getting started" information about fly fishing for species "beyond" trout, both beginners and advanced fly fishers will find plenty of useful material. I've found that expanding my customers' fishing horizons has rekindled many a flagging interest level. I hope you are encouraged as well.

Many of the fly patterns are of my design or incorporate modifications to existing patterns. Some are from other fly tyers and fishermen who have generously let me share their work in the hope that our collective experience can help make your fishing as rewarding as ours has been.

Good luck, and have fun fishing,

Joe Bruce

Chapter 1

THE SMALLMOUTH BASS

The adage "pound for pound the best fighting fish that swims" surely was made for the smallmouth bass. These broad-bodied fish never give up the battle until they are lifted from the water. The cold waters that are part of their life style might have something to do with it, but of all the bass family, the smallie is the gladiator of the species.

These fish can live for twenty years in the colder northern waters or for as few as ten years in the south; but the biggest of the smallmouth live where water temperatures allow for a longer growing season. The world record, an eleven pound brute, came from Dale Hollow Reservoir in Tennessee. A northern fish of five pounds is a trophy.

Wherever you pursue these great fish, be it the southern lakes, the rivers of Virginia, Maryland or Pennsylvania or the lakes and

Joe, in his earliest days of fly fishing.

rivers of the north, they are no pushovers and are made to be taken on the fly rod.

I have chased smallmouth bass since I was thirteen, and have used a fly rod for them since age sixteen. I still have to rate the smallie as one of my favorite fish. I have fished from Virginia to Canada for them and continue to make ten to twenty trips a year to fish for the bronzeback. During this time, I've developed a pretty good idea of what flies and techniques are most productive.

Nature of the Smallmouth Bass

The spread of the smallmouth to the east coast can be linked to the American Railroad. The original range was in the Ohio Valley river basin to Lake Ontario. The range was extended by wide planting of the fish from buckets hung under railroad cars

Smallmouth bass may have been originally stocked from this very bridge.

11

Railroads always follow rivers and streams.

Joe is still catching them on a fly today.

Measuring a "big un" before his release.

and dumped over bridge trestles. The stock in the Potomac River system were transplanted from the Ohio River by way of the Baltimore and Ohio Railroad as it moved over the Allegheny Mountains. As we know, they thrived well over the years despite flooding and droughts.

In lakes, they like clear, deep cold waters; in the rivers and streams, they like water flowing over gravel and rocks that aerate the water.

The smallmouth bass matures at about age three in the north to as early as two years in the south. They spawn from sometime in April to as late as June in the northern waters. Spawning takes place when the water temperature reaches from 60 to 70 degrees. Unlike the largemouth, smallmouth have no parental instinct. The fry leave the nest days after hatching to hide in any available cover. There they feed on minute crustaceans and later graduate to insect larvae, crawfish and other fish.

"Lipping" a nice smallie.

My wife, Barbara, will fly fish for smallmouth every change she gets.

14

Food and Prey

As they grow, their food preference also grows. The young-of-the-year minnows are fair game, as are sunfish and crappie in the lakes, and sculpins, minnows and crawfish in rivers and streams.

A calm day, good company (Barb with Bob Clouser, the originator of the Clouser's Deep Minnow) and fish.

Smallmouth bass and crawfish go together like cake and ice cream. Crawfish and smallmouth bass immediately bring the image of rocky waters, the bass looking around the rocks in the evening, searching in the shallows for their prey.

The first fly pattern I used to imitate a crawfish was a fly created by Ben Schley, a biologist for the U.S. Bureau of Fisheries doing long-term studies of the smallmouth bass in West Virginia.

One of Ben's favorite rivers, and where a vast majority of his data came from, was the Cacapon River, which flows into the upper Potomac River. Over the years of studying the stomach contents of the bass, it became evident that smallies over 10 inches preferred crawfish as their main diet.

Chapter 2

TACKLE

Rods

Depending on the usual size of the fish in your area, and upon your fishing inclinations, rods can run from 4-weight to 8-weight. We'll explain this more a little later. They should be from 8-1/2 to 9 feet long. Along with increased casting leverage, the longer rods will give you better lifting qualities than will shorter ones. Why is this? Generally as a rod gets longer, it needs a little heavier butt to carry its rated line weight. The length has absolutely nothing to do with wading deep or sitting in a canoe. Customers often come in the shop thinking that they need longer rods because of these conditions, but what they really need to do is improve their back cast.

I'm not going to go into the art of casting any more than to say that the fly line will always go in the direction that you speed up and come to a stop on your forward or backcast. If your backcast is directed down, then the line will hit the water behind you. Stop the tip in an upward direction, and the line will not hit the water. I sometimes demonstrate this by sitting on the ground with the forward section of a four-piece rod, casting sidearm, and the line will not hit the ground unless it is directed there.

Getting back to rods, any of the modern graphite rods will get the job done. As far as fast or moderate tip actions are concerned, the preference is up to the individual. They both can be fine tools. Obviously, different rod actions will feel different when you cast. If you are buying a new rod, you *must* try them out first. Different rods will definitely work better for different people. What your buddies recommend may be fine for them, but may not be the best for you. *You're* the one who will be using it!

To quote Lefty Kreh, "Elephants eat peanuts, but they don't make a living by doing it." What Lefty is referring to is that a large fish wants a larger meal. If you desire a shot at a bigger fish I would suggest using a 7- or 8-weight outfit. This will allow the use of larger wind-resistant flies or heavier weighted flies to dredge the bottom of the deeper holes. Of course, if you are concentrating on areas where the fish are smaller, and you won't be using large flies, then a 4- to 6-weight rig will be more suited to the quarry.

Reels

Here is where you can save some money. Any reel that will hold the fly line and some backing is adequate. Bass seldom make long, searing runs that require a super-smooth drag and 200 yards of backing. I sometimes carry two rods with me on the water while I'm wading, one rod rigged with floating line and the other with a sink-tip line. Since one of the reels is usually submerged for lengths of time, I prefer reels with drag systems that are not comprised of cork (which can absorb water).

System I or System II reels made by Scientific Angler, Pflueger, J. Ryall Reels, and Crown II reels by Cortland are some

I don't eat many fish, but fly rods. . . now that's a delicacy.

A nineteen-inch smallie from Lake Ontario.

reels that use a composite material as a drag. These range in price from $40 to $225, depending on reel size and contruction.

Finishes aren't a big concern in freshwater, so any of the finishes available on the above reels are okay. Painted versus anodized isn't a factor, though the anodized finishes will hold up better in the long run.

Now let's look at a more important part of the tackle system — one that doesn't always get the attention it deserves.

Lines

You should invest your money in the best lines that you can afford. Depending on whether you are fishing a lake or wading a river, you will need different lines to get the job done. I will discuss each useful line for these conditions.

No matter where you will fish for smallmouth, you will need a weight-forward floating line. A standard weight-forward line is adequate. A bass taper is *not* a must. The difference between the two lines is that the bass taper will have a shorter front taper than the standard weight-forward for carrying larger wind-resistant flies or bugs through the air. Again, this decision is a personal one on which line is best for you. You may want to discuss your requirements with your local fly-shop personnel. Whichever line you buy, try and buy the top or nearest the top brand of line you can afford. Better lines have harder finishes and this aids in making longer casts. They will float better, and also last longer than a less expensive line.

Have you ever tried using sink-tip lines? If not, you are missing out on a truly effective line for nearly any kind of fishing in rivers and streams. I use these lines for 90 percent of my fishing when I'm wading.

Many fisherman are afraid of sinking lines because they think they are hard to cast and because they can't see the fish hit the fly. Sink-tips rather then full-sinking lines lessen both these problems.

A 5-foot sink-tip is my first choice of sinking lines. The two line manufacturers of this sink-tip are Cortland Line Co. and Teeny

You never have enough flies.

Nymph Lines. They come in weights from 3 to 10. Cortland lines start from 5-weight up. Both have very fast sink rates at 6-1/2 to 7 inches per second.

I feel that this line gives the best control. First, it becomes obvious that with only a 5-foot sink-tip to deal with, the ability to

Be sure to wet your hands before handling a fish.

not only control the depth to which the line will sink, but the ability to control the drift is a lot easier to achieve.

Let's take a look at the water column and see some of the advantages of the sink-tip line. The water column has many different water speeds. The water at the top is the fastest, the water in the middle can be slower than the top, and the bottom can be faster than the middle, but maybe not as fast as the top. As you see, there are many forces being applied to the line in a single drift.

With the use of a typical strike indicator and split-shot combination, which has been used for years, you can see that a loop can form in the water column causing the fly to be either lifted off the bottom or weighted so heavily that the ability to control and cast the rig is greatly hampered. Also, the ability to add life to the fly is taken away by the split-shot. When you lift the rod, you may move the shot, but not move the fly. The fly just tends to keep sliding under the last split-shot. The point from the last split-shot to the fly is *dead space*, meaning that with this combination a fish

Rocks, ledges and eddys . . . smallmouth waters.

A lunch break with friends on the Susquehanna River.

can pick up the fly and spit it out without ever moving the split-shot, in turn not moving the strike indicator. You'll never know that a fish hit.

The sink-tip will help eliminate some of these negatives. First, with the sink-tip the faster water at the surface is not so much a factor. The sink-tip will be below this point and by mending the floating portion of line either upstream or down, you can make adjustments to help eliminate drag. Also, by lifting the rod tip and slowly dropping the tip as the line drifts downstream, you can keep in contact with the fly and impart a lifelike swimming or struggling movement. For a more in-depth explanation, see the chapter on fishing techniques.

If drift fishing in a boat or canoe, I find that a longer sinking line with a slower sink rate is a good choice. A 10-foot or longer tip with a sink rate around 3-1/2 to 4 inches per second will help keep the fly down as the craft drifts down-current. I sometimes make up these sinking lines by cutting a double taper full-sinking fly line and attaching this to a floating shooting line. The head should be around 35 feet. This setup will allow casts in the 80- to

A variety of suitable leaders and tippet spools.

100-foot range. Usually in these situations I'm casting across-stream and stripping the fly back to the boat, much like retrieving a spinner. Since the craft and fly line are traveling at the same rate of speed, this is much the same as stripping the line on a lake.

Just as a quick recap, a floating line is a basic necessity and a 5-foot or so sink-tip line for wading or boating will round out your fly line arsenal.

Leaders

Leaders need not be complicated for smallmouth fishing. For the floating lines, a 7-1/2 to 9-foot leader tapered to 6 lb. or 10 lb.

27

tippet is about right for 90 percent of your top water or subsurface fishing, unless, of course, you are using dry flies; then the proper tippet would be appropriately smaller, say 4x or 5x.

A simple and effective leader can be constructed with the "rules of halves." This is a simple formula that was developed by Lefty Kreh. The formula will allow you to develop any length leader. Start with any length butt and reduce the next piece by half. Continue reducing by halves for each additional section until you reach the tippet. Say you want a leader around ten feet: start with 4 feet of 25 lb. test, next tie on 2 feet of 20 lb., then 1 foot of

15 lb. test and complete the leader with 3 feet of tippet around 10 lb. (or 2x). This leader will roll over very well, and will allow you to cast a streamer or popper.

Leaders for the sink-tips are even simpler. Just add a 4-foot piece of appropriate tippet material (4x to 2x) and you are in business. A longer leader actually has an effect which is just the opposite of what you want with a sink-tip. With a long leader the monofilament tends to float, defeating the reason that you are using the sink-tip in the first place, which is to get the fly to the bottom. Even with a sinking fly the long monofilament will affect the descent rate of the fly. Smallies (indeed, most fish) are not particularly leader shy when the whole thing (line-tip, leader and fly) is all underwater. Keep the leader short and enjoy more fishing success.

Chapter 3
FLIES AND PATTERNS

There are an endless number of smallmouth fly patterns. You may like some for certain areas, or it may just be that you have confidence in a particular fly pattern that you use all the time. There are many patterns intended for other species that will have great success with smallmouth, maybe by just changing sizes or colors. By taking a Royal Wulff dry fly that is associated with trout fishing and changing the size to a number eight dry fly hook you have a good surface fly for smallmouth bass. There are many others.

The following flies and patterns are ones that I have had good success with over the years. Some patterns are old standbys, some are creations of mine or of my fishing partners and some are modifications to existing patterns. For *The Fisherman's Edge* patterns we will describe and illustrate the flies and provide tying instructions. They are time-tested and should be part of your arsenal of flies. We will also provide tying instruction for some additional flies that you might not be familiar with.

Surface Flies

Poppers. I like sizes running from 8 to 4. Colors can run the gamut from plain old white to chartreuse. Some with rubber legs should also be carried. Sometimes these are irresistible to the bass. Frog colored poppers will also do the trick.

Elk Hair Caddis are flies I always carry for use on the surface. There has been many a time on the river that the bass are
only interested in the insects that are floating down the current,
and a assortment of elk hairs can save the day. Gray or Olive Elk
hairs in sizes 14 to 18 will do the job.

Improved Sofa Pillows are a Western pattern that work wonders when the bass are chasing food on or near the surface. This large bushy fly might look like a moth, grasshopper or dragon fly to the bass; whatever they think it is, the surface will erupt when they are chasing it.

IMPROVED SOFA PILLOW

Hook: TMC 200R, Mustad 9672, sizes 4 to 8

Thread: Orange flat waxed nylon

Tail: Natural elk

Rib: Fine gold oval wire

Body: Orange dubbing or yarn

Hackle: Palmered brown or furnace

Wing: Elk

Hackle: Two brown hackles

◆ TYING INSTRUCTIONS

1. Place hook in vise and attach the thread behind eye and advance to bend of hook.

2. Tie in a small bunch of elk hair at this point. Ten to fifteen strands is about right. Trim butts and advance thread back to bend of hook.

3. Tie in the orange yarn and leave hanging.

4. Tie in ribbing and furnace hackle and advance thread to 3/8" back from the hook eye.

5. Wind body material to thread and tie off and cut.

6. Wind hackle to same point and tie off and cut. Do the same thing with the ribbing.

7. Take a small bunch of elk hair and place the wing on top and tie down and trim butts. The wing should extend to the bend of the hook.

8. Attach the two hackles in front of the elk hair wing and take one at a time and wind to the hook eye, leaving enough room for a head.

9. Cut off tips, form head and apply head cement.

This a great pattern for skating a fly across the surface. The bass will chase this fly with great enthusiasm.

There are many standard surface flies that will work for smallies. Just tie them in larger sizes from as small as 12, up to size six. These generally are taken as moths or hoppers, and the bass see these as a high protein meal. It's not a meal they normally will pass up.

Sub-Surface Flies

The following are a few flies that work just under the surface or when casting over shallow water. There are many more that might work for you, but these have consistently produced for me.

It's funny how two people, Lefty and myself, who love to fish for smallmouth, came to the same problem-solving decision. A large, bright fly will bring a strike near the surface, even when the fish are not really taking food off the surface. For me it was the White Zonker with a silver (or sometimes gold) body and for the "living legend," it was a Lefty's Red & White.

Lefty's Red & White Streamer is a bushy, undulating style subsurface streamer that will get the "big-uns" off the bottom. It's also a great fly to skate through the rapids, and it works well on saltwater flats too.

LEFTY'S RED & WHITE STREAMER

Hook: Mustad #3366, size 2 to 6

Thread: Fire-orange flat waxed nylon

Tail: White marabou

Tinsel: Silver Flashabou & pearl Krystal Flash

Head: Red Flash Chenille

◆ TYING INSTRUCTIONS

1. Place hook in vise and attach thread behind eye. Wind thread back toward hook bend about half the hook shank.

2. Attach a large bunch of white marabou at this point by throwing two loose wraps around the marabou and slowly tightening the thread as you slowly let the marabou slide around the hook shank. This should be evenly dispersed. The marabou should extend past the hook bend about twice the hook length.

3. Take three strands each of the flashabou and tie in on each side of the marabou, letting it extend about 3/8" past the marabou. Also tie in a few strands of Krystal Flash, the same length as the Flashabou.

4. At this point tie in about 4" of flash chenille and wind to back of hook eye leaving enough room to form a head.

5. Form head, whip finish and apply head cement.

Zonkers are another of the good subsurface flies that work well. This Australian pattern with the rabbit strip wing really undulates in the current during the retrieve, working well with both silver or gold bodies. Try either one until you get a strike. Perhaps these flies represent the young-of-the-year suckers, fall fish or carp that roam the waters in the early summer through the fall. Sizes 2 to 8 on 3x long streamer hooks are about right.

White Zonker

Hook:	Mustad #79850, sizes 2 thru 8
Thread:	Fire-orange flat waxed nylon
Body:	Silver or gold mylar tubing over cardboard body frame
Throat:	Red Krystal Flash
Wing:	White rabbit zonker strip
Head:	Fire-orange flat waxed nylon

♦ TYING INSTRUCTIONS

1. Place hook in vise and attach thread in back of hook eye and wrap back to bend of hook.

2. Take a piece of cardboard, (a business card is perfect) and cut out an underbody for the mylar tubing. See illustration below.

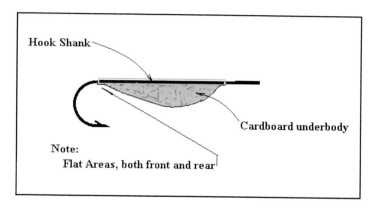

Hook Shank

Cardboard underbody

Note:
Flat Areas, both front and rear

By folding the card lengthwise you will be able to get a few bodies from each card. Set the body over the hook shank and trim the body where necessary for the size of hook.

Trim the card to leave little flat areas on each end. Here is where you can tie down the body, hard to the hook shank. You can wind back and forth over the body, but only pull hard at the tie-on points. Finish wrapping the underbody at the bend of the hook.

3. Whip finish at this point and leave about twelve inches of thread hanging.

4. Cut a piece of mylar tubing about one and a half inches longer than the hook shank. Remove core and slide tubing over underbody. Leave 1/8" of tubing hanging over

hook eye. While holding the tubing in place take your thread bobbin and attach the thread over the body and hook shank. After securing the thread, cut off the tag. This tie-in point should be about 1/4" behind the hook eye. This will give you enough room for the beard and rabbit wing. This fly imitates a minnow, which has a large head.

5. Invert hook in the vise and take about 12 to 15 strands of red Krystal Flash and tie down at this point.
Extend throat about 1/4" from hook shank and cut off.

6. Return hook to its upright position and take a piece of zonker strip and tie down on top of the hook shank opposite the throat. The skin side goes against the hook shank. Finish the head at this point and cut thread.

7. Take your bodkin and start picking out the weave of the mylar tubing until you get to the hanging thread. Grasp the mylar tubing and pull back, stretching the tubing over the underbody. Take the hanging thread and wrap around the hook shank tying down the tubing. Attach hackle pliers to the hanging thread. Grasp the rabbit strip and pull it back to the hook bend. Take your bodkin and separate the hair on the skin where the tying thread is hanging. Wet your fingers and moisten the separation of hair at this point to facilitate tying down the skin without capturing too many rabbit hairs.

8. Tie down zonker strip and whip finish and tie off. Apply head cement to both wraps.

Note: If you cannot perform a hand whip finish, tie down the mylar tubing and rabbit strip at the bend of the hook first and then proceed to tie the pattern toward the head and finish the fly.

The "B" Damsel is a fly that was developed by one of my best fishing buddies, Bill Kollmer. The B is for Bill and the damsel is because the first time that I saw the pattern, I told Bill it looks like a damsel nymph.

The origin of this pattern is as an offshoot of the *Bruce's PK40* (a multihatch fly I designed for the Potomac). This pattern is illustrated in the Bottom Bouncing section of this book.

Though this fly is weighted over the entire length of the hook, it is included with the subsurface flies because of the effectiveness of the fly when moving to the surface on the swing from an across and down style cast. The fish seem to hit it at the top of the swing.

This pattern is also effective when there is more than one hatch coming off. It has accounted for other species of fish besides the smallmouth. We have taken trout, largemouth bass, crappie and bluegill with it.

As stated, at first glance the fly resembles a damsel nymph; we use the fly both in a dark phase and also a light phase by changing the back and the color of the dubbing. The dubbing need not be anything special, just use a material that tends to absorb water to help it sink.

"B" DAMSEL

Hook: Mustad #9672 - size 8

Thread: Flat waxed nylon-brown or black

Weight: .015 lead

Tail: Brown and olive marabou or brown and orange

           equal amounts of both

Back: Swiss straw-brown, green or orange

Ribbing: Medium oval gold tinsel

Hackle: Furnace or dark ginger

Body: Any olive or orange dubbing or Buggy Yarn

◆ TYING INSTRUCTIONS

1. Attach thread behind hook eye and advance to bend of hook.

2. Attach lead at hook point and wrap 13-14 turns toward hook eye.

3. Tie in equal amounts of two marabous. Marabou should be about 1/4" longer than the hook length.

4. Tie in the Swiss straw at the bend of the hook. This will form a back covering the whole length of the hook shank, so leave enough material to accomplish this.

5. Tie in the hackle at this point as well as the tinsel.

6. Apply dubbing or yarn to the thread and start wrapping toward the hook eye. The dubbing need not be tied in heavy; a medium size body for this fly should be approximately twice the thickness of the hook shank. Advance thread and dubbing to about 3/16" behind hook eye.

Remember you have to finish the fly with the hackle, tinsel and back behind the hook eye, so plenty of room is needed.

7. Wind the tinsel toward the hook eye, spacing the wraps equally as you approach the tie-off point.

8. Palmer the hackle between the tinsel and tie off.

9. Pull the Swiss straw over the whole back and tie off behind the hook eye.

10. Finish head, whip finish and apply head cement.

Another pattern that is included with the subsurface flies, but by no means is limited to this portion of the water column is the *Bendback*. Bendback style flies are flies that ride with the hook up, so they can be used in very shallow water as well as fished through structure without hanging up. A slight bending of the hook shank, and tying the materials on so as to cover the hook point makes the fly semi-weedless. This is actually a tying style rather than a particular pattern.

Bottom-Bouncers

I feel these are the top producing flies in a fisherman's arsenal for the simple reason that fish spend 90 percent or more of their time on or near the bottom. It stands to reason that a fly that stays in this same area will catch fish.

It's amazing that fishermen refrain from fishing these patterns or will only resort to them when they haven't had any success on the surface. Learn to fish deep and your catch ratio will soar.

The following patterns are my favorites. Three of these are my creations that were developed with the smallmouth in mind, but they have taken many other species of fish as well.

The Bruce's Crystal Bugger came about after the first time I saw "flash Chenille," and immediately realized its potential. Over the years I have developed a series of flies using this material. With the *Crystal Bugger* alone I have taken 31 different species of fish by just changing sizes and color combinations, but the first fish was a smallmouth bass.

If you aren't familiar with flash chenille, it is a chenille type material that is available in either a pearl glimmer or regular shades. This Mylar type material is woven around multiple strands of very fine nylon to create a cactus type of a look. Some tyers even refer to this material by the name cactus chenille. It comes in an array of colors. My favorites are chartreuse, peacock, pearl, black, golden olive and tan. Working with flash chenille is no different than working with any other style of chenille. I find this material to be an especially effective product to work with.

As mentioned, my first use of the material was for small-mouth. I tied two streamer style patterns using chartreuse flash chenille for the body and took them to the Potomac to one of my favorite stretches of the river. I had been fishing for about an hour in an area that I knew like the back of my hand, and wasn't setting the world on fire. The water was low and clear. I tied on one of these new creations, which by all standards was bright and gaudy. On the first cast I had a hard hit and proceeded to land my first smallmouth of the day. The next cast produced the same thing, and on the third cast a fish broke me off. I tied the other crystal bugger on the same light tippet that I was using and had the same results with this fly; three fish on and the third one breaking me off. From then on I have never been to any smallmouth waters without a good supply of these flies.

The following pattern description is the original one that I used on the Potomac River.

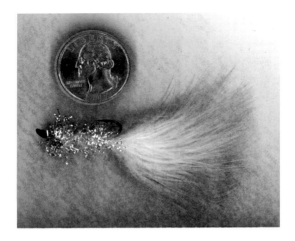

BRUCE'S CRYSTAL BUGGER

Hook: Mustad #9672 or equal-size 6 to 10

Thread: 3/0 flat waxed nylon or monocord (I like fire-orange flat waxed nylon)

Lead Eyes: #6 & #8-1/50oz, #10-1/100oz

Tail: Yellow marabou

Body: Chartreuse Flash Chenille or glimmer Flash Chenille

Head: Flat waxed nylon or monocord

◆ TYING INSTRUCTIONS

1. Place hook in vise and attach thread behind hook eye. Advance thread to bend of hook.

2. Tie in marabou and tie in flash chenille. Marabou should be at least the length of the hook.

3. Advance the thread to about 3/16" from the back of the hook eye.

4. Tie in the lead eye by wrapping in a figure-eight pattern

over the eye and hook shank and then by lashing the eye in by wrapping the thread over the hook shank and under the eye on both sides of the lead eye. This will anchor the eye in place. If you would like, you can add a drop of head cement on these wraps.

5. Wrap the flash chenille around the hook shank advancing to the back of the lead eye. Wrap the chenille around the lead eye in the same figure-eight pattern that you used to secure the lead eye. Two wraps around each side will do. Then make one wrap in front of the eye toward the hook eye.

6. Tie off chenille and form head, whip finish and apply head cement.

This has all the properties that a good fly needs; it is quick and easy to tie, is durable and catches fish. What else could you ask for?

My favorite color combinations for smallmouth are chartreuse body with yellow tail, chartreuse with white tail, pearl with white tail, peacock with olive tail or brown, and brown with orange tail.

Normally the strike is anything but subtle, making the fly a good pattern to start with if you haven't had too much experience with fishing on the bottom.

Bruce's PK 40 is another of my favorite bottom bouncer patterns.

The first thing people want to know is, "what the heck is a PK 40?" It all started with fly fishermen coming into the shop asking about the Potomac Killer that they had been hearing about. I thought that I could at least come up with a better name than the Potomac Killer, so I decided to call it the PK 40. The PK was the abbreviation, and 40 was my age at the time I developed the fly.

The fly is a maverick of sorts. It looks like a regular nymph from the front, but the tail looks like a set of claws from a crawfish.

This fly was the result of a lot of years on the Potomac trying to develop a fly that would work most of the time during multi-hatch situations or when fish are chasing the young-of-the-year minnows, or when there is no apparent activity at all.

The PK is a long fly. The tail is as long as the whole hook length. This has two purposes. First, the length and the easy movement of the rabbit looks like the claws of a crawfish, and secondly, it also looks like the tail of a minnow. The tail, when the fly falls through the current, tends to ride upwards and mimics the defensive posture of the crawfish going back to the bottom. The body is extremely bright, which acts as an attractor or stimulator.

As you can see this fly was designed to help us when there is not a specific type of fishing pattern in evidence.

BRUCE'S PK 40

Hook: Mustad #9672 - size 8

Thread: Red monocord

Tail: Natural rabbit

Weight: .015 lead wire

Ribbing: Medium oval gold tinsel

Body: Fly-Rite-inchworm green

Wing Case: Peacock herl

Legs: Brown or ginger hackle

Thorax: Inchworm green Fly-Rite

Head: Monocord - red

◆ TYING INSTRUCTIONS:

1. Insert hook in vise and attach thread behind hook eye and advance thread to bend of hook. Start wrapping lead at hook point and continue wrapping forward to about 1/4" from back of hook eye. Next lay a piece of lead on each side of the wrapped lead and tie down.

2. Advance thread to bend of hook and tie in rabbit, cut from a zonker strip. Tie this heavy and as long as the hook length. I sometimes tie in two bunches to achieve the right thickness.

3. Tie in oval tinsel.

4. Apply dubbing to the thread; this also should be on the heavy side. Wind dubbing to the end of the body lead near the hook eye.

5. Spiral the tinsel ribbing forward, ending at the dubbing.

6. Tie in ten strands of peacock herl, and then the brown or ginger hackle.

7. Again dub the thread and wrap to behind hook eye, leaving enough room for the hackle, wing case and head.

8. Wrap the hackle and tie off. Three wraps are enough.

9. Pull peacock herl over and tie down in back of hook eye and form head.

10. Whip finish head and apply head cement.

The PK 40 has proven itself in all the smallmouth waters that I have fished, as well as in the small streams entering the bigger waters. I have also had good success with this fly on the Delaware River taking American shad.

Think of a crawfish and your thoughts will conjure up the image of a smallmouth bass making it a meal. These two go together like cake and ice cream. My *Crystal Crawfish* will make these images come to life.

This is another fly using flash chenille as a body. The strikes come hard using this fly, reinforcing the fact that the smallie also takes this pattern as a crawfish.

I tie the crystal crawfish in four color combinations, tan, rootbeer (burnt orange), brown and orange. All these are good producers. I also tie the fly on stainless steel hooks after Lefty Kreh embarrassed me by calling the rootbeer color crawfish a good *crab pattern*. Well, since he felt this was a crab, I would tie it in stainless, just in case. Guess what? The pattern has been used as a crab on the flats of Florida and the Caribbean and indeed has taken bonefish as well as permit. Thanks, Lefty.

50

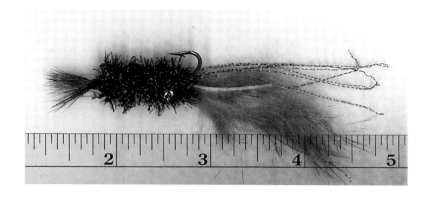

BRUCE'S CRYSTAL CRAWFISH

Hook: Mustad #34007-size 4

Thread: Flat waxed nylon, fire-orange

Claws: Natural rabbit zonker strip

Antenna: 4 to 6 strands of copper Krystal Flash

Body: Flash Chenille

Eyes: 1/50 oz. lead eyes

Tail: Natural deer body hair

◆ TYING INSTRUCTIONS

1. Place hook in vise and attach the tread behind hook eye and advance to bend of hook.

2. Tie in lead eye at a point right above the hook barb. Add a drop of cement if you want to.

3. Tie in about 6" of flash chenille behind the lead eye toward the hook bend.

4. Tie in the Krystal Flash. The strands should be about 1- 1/2 times longer than the hook length.

5. Cut two pieces of rabbit zonker strips a little longer than 1/4". Be careful not to cut the fur off the skin. Carefully slide the scissors under the fur to cut the skin only.

6. Place the two rabbit strips skin to skin and tie down in the same place that the Krystal Flash was tied.

7. Turn the hook over in the vise and wind the thread to the back of the hook eye. Even a small bunch of deer body hair in a stacker. Extend the tips over the hook eye about 1/4" and bind down the rest of the deer hair and butts on the top of the hook shank to the back of the lead eye. This point is the area closest to the hook eye. Cut excess and advance thread to back of hook eye.

8. Again turn hook over in the vise and start wrapping flash chenille around the lead eye in a figure-eight pattern. Two wraps each way around eye is about right. Continue wrapping chenille to back of hook eye and tie off.

9. Whip finish and apply head cement.

Another fly that cannot be overlooked is one of the most popular fly patterns for many freshwater species, the *wooly bugger*. Use either brown chenille with brown marabou or black chenille with black marabou. Both flies use grizzly hackle palmered over the chenille. They should be weighted heavily to get to the bottom fast. Try sizes from 6 to 12s. Also, your arsenal should include some wooly buggers in white and in yellow. For some reason the yellow wooly bugger can turn a bad day into a great day. This fly has been the answer on some of

those occasions when the other standard fish-catchers aren't catching. Tying instructions aren't necessary here; just look in any fly tying book and you will find the wooly bugger.

These flies are most likely taken as crawfish, hellgrammites, minnows or leaches, depending on what part of the country you are fishing. Nevertheless, these are flies that should be added to your fly box.

The list of bottom bouncing flies couldn't be complete without the *Clouser's Deep Minnow*. Beyond a doubt it's the most effective underwater fly around. Originated by Robert Clouser of Middletown, Pennsylvania, this fly has become the *must* fly for just about every species of fish that swim.

I'm lucky enough to live only a two hour drive from Bob, and have had the pleasure of fishing and chatting with this fine gentleman numerous times. On the river, we have fished his creations with great success. Following are Bob's *Clouser Crayfish,* and his recipe for *"The Baby Bass,"* one of his famous Clouser's Deep Minnows.

Bob Clouser, right at home on the Susquehanna River.

53

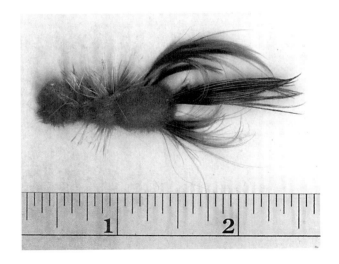

 CLOUSER'S CRAYFISH

Hook: Mustad #38941 or #9672 streamer hook, size 4 or 6

Thread: Tan waxed 3/0 Monocord

Weight: .025 lead wire

Antennae: 6 to 8 ringneck pheasant tail fibers

Nose: 6 to 8 hen mallard breast fibers

Under head: 1 cm cork cylinder, split in half, cut this to 5mm

Carapace: 12mm wide strip of Furry Foam, olive/brown

Body: Dubbing combination of white sparkle yarn and
          green wool. Antron blend will also work

Pincers: 2 layers ringneck rump feathers, under hen mallard
          flank feathers

Swimmerettes: Bleached grizzly or barred ginger hackle

◆ TYING INSTRUCTIONS

1. Insert hook in vise, attach the tying thread behind the hook eye and advance to bend of hook. Lash one piece of .025 lead on each side of hook shank. Advance thread to hook bend.

2. Tie in ringneck tail fibers as antennae. Over this, tie in a small bunch of hen mallard breast fibers as the "nose."

3. Tie in cork over head. Apply head cement to help secure. This cork is only needed for size 4 hooks or larger to keep the crayfish upright on the drop. On smaller hooks this can be eliminated.

4. Tie in Furry Foam strip at hook bend and let it hang.

5. Apply enough dubbing to the thread to cover the cork.

6. Cut a "V" shape in the ringneck rump and hen mallard feathers. Tie in the two layers of ringneck, then apply the hen mallard so that the "V" is on each side of the head to form pincers.

7. Cover this area with dubbing and pull Furry Foam over and tie down behind pincers. Leave Foam hanging.

8. Tie in bleached grizzly or barred ginger hackle at this point. Advance thread to behind hook eye.

9. Apply dubbing to thread and wind back to the hackle tie-in point and let the bobbin hang.

10. Grasp hackle and palmer it over the dubbed body to behind the hook eye and tie off.

11. Pull the rest of the Furry Foam over the body and rib with the hanging thread to behind the eye. Tie off the thread and whip finish.

12. Pull the tag end of the Furry Foam over the hook eye and by using your fingernail, cut through the Foam at the eye and push Foam over eye. Cut the Foam about 1/16" in front of the hook eye.

13. Carefully trim the edges of the Foam to round them; this will keep the fly from spinning in the current.

14. Apply cement to the finish wraps.

Bob and friend.

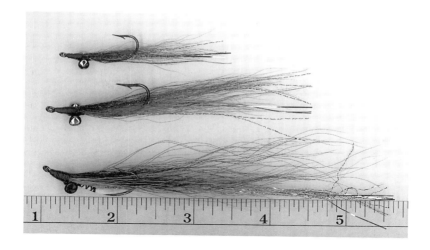

No tying instructions are given for the *Clouser's Deep Minnows*, since they are standard patterns and can be found in nearly all pattern books. The following instructions only show the materials needed and are in the sequence to use in tying the fly.

 CLOUSER'S DEEP MINNOW — "BABY BASS"

Belly: White bucktail

Middle: Green or olive bucktail

Flash: Bronze or copper Flashabou with gold Krystal Flash

Back: Brown bucktail

To round out the Clouser selections, my other favorite *Clouser's Deep Minnows* are brown and orange, and chartreuse and white. With these three minnow imitations you should do well. Use sizes running from 4 to 10, tied on streamer hooks.

"Catch and Return" fishing is stock in our future.

Chapter 4

FISHING TECHNIQUES

General Information

Fishing situations change not only from day to day, but sometimes from minute to minute. There are hundreds of ways to fish a fly. The following techniques are some that I have had repeated success with over the years, but by no means are they the only way to fish a given pattern or type of water.

Throughout our discussion, keep in mind that there are contrasts between fishing moving water (streams and rivers) while wading and while in a boat or float tube. The two situations are different because while wading, the current is moving past you

A good-looking break in the current. Guess where the fish will be?

and is affecting the action of the fly line. In a boat, you're moving at the same speed as the current, and so is the line; it will be much less affected by the flow of the water.

A good piece of general information to file away in your memory is that *Smallmouth bass in rivers and streams tend to move upstream, or at least across stream,* in going to feeding areas. They do the same thing in the spring to spawn. How does this af-

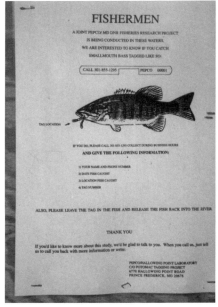

Tagging programs help the Department of Natural Resources evaluate seasons and limits through this gathered data.

fect fishing? In a nutshell it means the best water will usually be to the side or upstream of the deeper pools. This doesn't necessary apply for very still running pools, but if there is a ledge in fast water, the fish will move above the ledge to intercept the food. This is especially true in warm summertime conditions.

Before we get started on other techniques, let's discuss a fishing pattern that usually isn't very successful, but is easy to fall into. That is, strip-retrieving the fly directly upstream toward you. Will you catch fish at times? Certainly, but generally these are smaller fish. Large fish do get caught at times, probably when migrating upstream and seeing the food for the first time. It works sometimes, but it's a low percentage retrieve. Minnows can swim upstream, so streamer patterns can be retrieved this way, but swimming a nymph upstream is not very natural.

If you are inclined to use this method, you will do better by moving the fly rod back and forth as you strip upstream, causing the streamer to move across the current. This is a much more realistic representation of a minnow's swimming pattern.

Shoreline structure always deserves a cast or two.

Late fall can be a time for large smallmouth.

Better Hookups

Probably the most frequently asked question in my fly shop is, "What can I do to catch more fish?" My answer is always the same, *SHARPEN YOUR HOOKS*. This is not the answer the customers are looking for (they want *more* fish), but after they are able to find fish, a sharp hook will put more of them on the line.

Many modern hooks claim to have sharper points. There are terms such as Laser sharpened, "Accura Point", chemically sharpened, etc. They *are*, in fact, sharper then a common hook, but, at least in the larger sizes, need to be sharper yet. They need to be honed to produce the right point.

A sharp hook is produced by triangulating the hook point. This is done with a small flat stone, a file, or a diamond hone with medium to fine grit. Triangulating is done by stroking the hook point first on one side (along-side the barb), then on the other, and finally by stroking the point opposite the hook barb. *All these strokes should be toward the bend of the hook,* not toward the point, and should be at a deep angle. Going toward the point tends to roll over the tip, actually forming a little curl.

A simple test to check hook sharpness is to touch the hook point to the top of your thumb nail. A properly sharpened hook will resist sliding, and will stick to the nail. While fishing, occasionally check your hook for sharpness by simply doing this thumb nail test. Hooks *do* get dull from encounters with rocks, bottom debris, fish's mouths, etc.

The next step for better hook sets is to bend down the hook barb. This allows deeper hook penetration because of the reduction of the point width. Few of us notice any increased tendency to lose fish (the better penetration off-sets the lack of a barb), and it certainly allows for easier release.

The last tip for better hook sets is how to use both the rod and your hands. First and foremost, the rod should always be pointing pretty much straight down the line; the word is *ALWAYS*. I can't

Always strip with the rod tip low.

Setting the hook and fighting fish should be done with the rod butt.

think of one situation where this wouldn't be the proper position for the rod tip. This gives you the ability to create a direct pull on the line to the fly. This pulling action is how you should initially set the hook, and is called a "line set" or "hand set." If you simply yank the line back toward your hips, it will give you the most power that you can impart to the hook. This type of set also has the advantage of keeping the fly in the strike zone in case you missed the fish. If you try to set the hook by lifting the rod tip, you move the fly over a longer distance and have less chance of giving the fish another shot at it.

Once you have hooked the fish, you can use the rod to ensure a solid hook set. I sometimes do this several times to make sure the hook is driven home. A proper rod set is done with the butt of the rod, not the tip. The tip is the weakest point on the rod and has the least amount of power. The most effective way to drive the hook home is by snapping your rod hand straight back, just passing your hips. Don't forget, your rod will *ALWAYS* be pointing down the line — not up in the air.

I recommend that you test the power of different rod angles at home. Run your line through the guides and have someone hold on to the end of it and stand fifteen feet or so away. Pull the rod tip up in the air toward the sky, and ask your partner how much pressure you are applying. Next, keep the rod tip low, pretty much down the line. Pull back with the rod butt and with your line hand, and ask the same question. Reverse positions with your partner and do the experiment again. You will be amazed at the difference in pressure. If you use a scale to measure the pounds generated, you might find as much as three times the force from a butt set compared to a tip set.

While we are talking about rod control, remember to always fight the fish with the rod not fully vertical. The same principles pertain as in setting the hook. If the tip is up in the air, you are applying virtually no pressure to the fish. It looks good in a picture, but you're not in complete control of that fish. A good rule of

A side view, showing the how hook set.

Rocks and gravel will hold crawfish.

thumb is to never have the rod butt perpendicular to the fish. Another strong fighting technique is to always have the rod pulling away from the direction of the fish's movement. By keeping the head of the fish turning against the pull of the rod, you will actually cause the fish to change direction. This tires it out, and moves it toward you each and every time it changes direction.

Covering the Water

Covering water thoroughly is the sign of a good and successful fisherman, be it on a river or a lake, underneath or on top. Finding structure and making repeated casts to the structure from different angles will spell success. *Patience is a virtue.*

While guiding on the Potomac, I found that some clients who only had fished small streams for trout were overwhelmed when confronted with a river that was hundreds of yards wide. To settle them down I would suggest that the first current break in front of them was the other side of the stream and we would fish that sec-

66

tion first, then move to the next break and fish that. Also, think of the water as a checkerboard and fish each grid one at a time, starting with the closest and farthest down below you and working the cast up and over, overlapping the previously fished water. This is *thoroughly* fishing the water.

Another advantage of fishing this checker board pattern and fishing the down stream positions first, is that if there is any congregation of fish in the area, a hooked fish will generally run down stream away from the other fish. Thus you can catch more fish in a given area without spooking fish further upstream from your first cast.

Where To Look

Before stepping into the water, first stop on the bank and look around a little bit. Do you see any fish activity? Are they raising? What are their raises like? Are they around rocks, below riffles, above the ledges or rocks? These are the kinds of indicators that will help you decide what type of tactics to use to take advantage of the particular behavior pattern.

On his way back to the river.

Smallmouth territory.

If the fish are active on the surface, are they jumping out of the water or are they just rolling on the surface? These two raises are totally different, and a popper or dry fly might *not* be the answer. If the bass is jumping out of the water, don't use a surface fly. These fish are taking emergers. Emergers are a stage in the life of an insect as it is rising toward the surface to hatch into a winged insect. The fish are taking them as they move through the water column. Since fish don't have brakes (Meineke or Midas won't get much business), their momentum carries them through the surface and into the air. I have listened to many fishermen describe leaping fish and their amazement that they wouldn't take anything on the surface. After understanding what is happening, they are better armed when they see this feeding pattern again.

If the fish are dimpling or rolling on the surface, *then* they can be taken with surface flies or poppers. Sometimes a more effective technique can be to fish a nymph or a cut-down dry fly just under the surface. This tactic is easily accomplished by putting line dressing on your leader down to about six inches short of the fly. Do not dress the fly, since this will allow it to float in the surface film or just a inch or two underneath. This imitates the emerging insect moving to the surface or caught in the surface film. It's an effective top water technique.

Let's look back to the question, "Do you see any fish activity?" Suppose there isn't. Where do you start? Sometimes this will depend on the season of the year. We'll provide more infor-

Bill Kollmer with a nice one.

mation about seasonal fishing techniques in Chapter 5, but here are some relevant high points.

In spring, the water is colder and the fish are sluggish. They don't feed as heavily or as often, but they will always be feeding where there is the least amount of current. This can be in back eddies behind rocks, islands, sandbars or below ledges. Anywhere that the speed of the current is diminished, the bait will congregate and so will the bass. Fishing the shore line can be the best choice. Try small wooly buggers and streamers. Fish thoroughly, with overlapping casts. In the colder water the fish aren't as aggressive, so repeated casts to the same general area will put more bend in your rod.

Late spring or summer will find the bigger fish resting above the ledges or in front of the rocks. These are good areas to concentrate on, because the bigger fish want to get the first crack at the food.

Fall will find the fish holding in deeper water. They generally will not be feeding in the mornings. The night temperatures have cooled the water, along with their metabolism. They tend to get more active as the sun starts to warm the surface water. Late morning through late afternoon is the best time to go after them.

What makes good fishing waters? The obvious answer would be the area that holds the most food. Why do certain areas hold more food? *They have shallow water flats near deep water.* In the shallows and along the water's edge is where the food chain begins. The microscopic foods that minnows and insects feed on are there. So are the larger crustaceans, such as freshwater shrimps or scuds and crayfish. Some flats will have small grass islands near the edges. They provide the homes and rearing spots for minnows and insects.

Watch these waters closely for activity from larger fish. Look for minnows jumping and running in all directions when a larger predatory fish attacks them. The larger fish move from their deeper water lairs, make blitz assaults to the shore, and then settle back to the edges of the deep water to wait for the minnows to re-join into small groups before attacking them again. Streamer flies such as

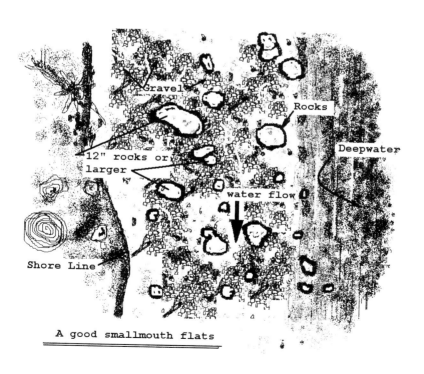

A good smallmouth flats

Clousers or bucktail flies work well here, as do wooly buggers. Poppers thrown into the melee will also bring a strike.

Not all flats are alike. Although most will hold bait and food, the best ones are those that have a generous scattering of stones around six to twelve inches across, along with a smattering of larger diameter rocks. Rocks of this size will give sanctuary to crayfish — that favorite food of the smallmouth bass. The rocks give the crayfish enough cover to dig their burrows to hide, lay eggs and rest until they are ready to look for food.

Such areas are prime fishing spots in the early evenings through dark. I fished an area like this on the Potomac River one mid-July with my wife, Barbara, and between us we had a great evening. This particular spot had deep water near some flats, and the flats had a mixture of rock and stone to about one foot in diameter. As the sun started off the water, the crayfish started moving and so did the smallmouth. Barb was fishing a popper where the deep water and the shallows met, casting out in the main channel and allowing the popper to drift down-current with slight twitches. I fished a popper out on the flats. We both did equally well. She caught the fish as they started their migration to the flats, and I caught them looking for food once they got there. The fishing was very much like fishing for bonefish on a salt-flat. I could see the wake of a fish as it came onto the shallows, and would cast slightly ahead of the wake. The bass would just keep coming and slurp up my offering. The water would explode as the fish charged off the

A good fishing buddy, Larry Meyer, with a more typical size smallie.

Most rivers have an access points. Looking for them in the off season will aid in your plan of attack.

flats to its deeper hideout. I could catch a few fish from an area, and then have to wait for it to settle down before they would come back to it. The water sometimes wasn't six inches deep. Although we had only twenty fish over twelve inches, we probably caught around fifty fish in a couple of hours. That's a pretty good evening on the Potomac.

Bob Clouser, who fishes the Susquehanna River, enjoys the same type of flats. We have fished these areas in the evenings together with similar results to the above story. Look for such flats, especially on a warm summer or early fall evening, and you too will be able to relate this same tale to your fishing buddies.

Since fishing isn't an exact science and no fish reads what writers write, they don't always do the logical thing. Sometimes evening fishing is good and sometimes not. Sometimes they will bite right through to pitch-black and other times they will stop three hours before dark. Experience will tell you when to go home, because it's all over with for that day. . . or is it?

Night Fishing

If night fishing is something that you might want to try, here are some tips and some precautions.

First and foremost, you should *be familiar with the waters you are fishing.* In unfamiliar waters you can get in trouble quickly, by stepping into a hole or getting tangled up in an underwater obstruction. Water can flow through a brushy obstruction, but you can't. Having a fishing partner with you at night isn't a bad idea. Also, let someone know where you are and approximately when you might be home. If you run late, call this person as soon as you can get to a telephone.

Now how about fishing at night? This is the time to catch the largest bass. It's their feeding time. They tend to be less cautious since there isn't much trouble coming from the air (such as eagles, herons and ospreys), but you still have to move quietly and slowly.

Even though this is their time to feed, they don't feed all night. You don't eat all day, do you? There will be slow periods during the night as there are during the day. Let's create a typical scenario to illustrate this:

The White Millers have been

hatching for two days. The hatch will start around an hour before dark or maybe after dark. There are clouds of insects flying, and bass are feeding on both the insects and the minnows chasing the insects. This lasts for a couple of hours. Did the fish feed for a couple of hours? Hardly. They fed for a while and than tapered off. Later in the night the previous night's Millers will be mating and dying, falling to the water, to become what are called "spinners." This might take place a few hours after the evening hatch or might happen at the same time. Either way, some fish will be feeding, others will be stopping. Sometime around three or four AM there could be a spinner fall from the current night's hatching. The fish will feed again. This is one reason that fishing in the morning after a miller hatch is slow; the fish just stopped feeding a couple of hours ago and they aren't hungry.

While fishing the Susquehanna on a September evening with a couple of buddies, the fish fed on crayfish for about an hour and a half. When I caught the first good smallmouth bass that evening (a sixteen incher), I looked at my watch; it was 8:05. I had been on the water since 7 PM and had only caught two small fish. When I left the water at 9:30, I had taken thirteen nice smallies up to seventeen and a half inches. All took a brown and orange *Crystal Bugger*, size 6, with a shorter than normal tail (which helps to eliminate short strikes). Any crayfish pattern would have worked. I have to point out that this was *in that magic area, deep water close to shallows, with twelve-inch rocks littering the bottom.* The fish were coming up in waves for the crayfish. No doubt, staying longer and waiting for the next group of bass coming onto the flats would have offered more of the same kind of fishing.

Night fishing can be worthwhile.

Surface Fishing

Here are three techniques for popper fishing:

1. When fishing a popper in a river, the first technique that I recommend is to *keep it moving*. This will take the aggressive fish. Cast across current and immediately start popping it back to you. This will allow you to cover a lot of water in a hurry. The style is akin to what the bass pros do during a tournament; that is, make long casts, cover a lot of water and take the most aggressive fish. I always start with this method to judge what the fish are doing at the time that I first hit the water. It's quick and is often the most effective way to fish. The proper way to do this is to cast 3/4 downstream and retrieve the fly until it's completely downstream of you. Pick up the popper and make the next cast a little more upstream than the first one. Continue doing this until you have fished the cast almost all the way upstream. This is an effective way to thoroughly cover a body of water.

2. Fish the popper with *pops and pauses* during the retrieve. This sometimes will trigger the fish which has heard the commotion and comes looking for the source. These fish will usually follow the popper a little downstream, and will take it on the next pop. I consider such fish to be a little less aggressive than the fish that take the continually moving popper. I have caught some of my best fish with this technique. Cover the water the same way as described above.

3. Fish the popper on a *nearly dead drift*. I use the same casting pattern, but only twitch the popper to add life to it. I am always amazed that fish will take this presenta-

tion with all the twigs, grass and debris floating down the river and can recognize the fly as some kind of food; but maybe that isn't what happens. I can't remember the last time that I saw a chartreuse bug floating down the river. I suspect that the eating-reaction is mostly from curiosity to see if such a thing might taste good.

Some of the same presentations that I use on poppers I also use on dry flies. High floating flies like the Elk Hair Caddis and the Improved Sofa Pillow can be dressed with dry fly floatant and skated across the current just like the poppers. This is a sight that fish are accustomed to with wind-blown insects on breezy days. This triggers an immediate take because the fish instantly has to take the fly or make the decision to let it pass downstream; there isn't time for a long look.

During heavy fly hatches I *don't* like to try and match the hatch. If there are thousands of insects on the water, the chance of the fish picking up yours is slim. My philosophy is that since the fish are already looking up, throw a pattern that is a little larger

Dams are man-made fish stops.

and different from the predominant insect, and the odds are that a fish isn't going to let that much protein drift on by without a try. It's not always successful, but I feel my chances are a little better than by using the strict "match the hatch" approach.

Sometimes during these hatches, sinking a dry fly just under the surface and stripping with a pause in between will work the fish up to a strike. This is best accomplished by applying floatant down your leader to about 6 inches from your fly. This will cause the fly to sit just under the surface much like a soft hackle fly does on a trout stream. A slight lifting of the rod tip will raise the fly up toward the surface like an emerging insect. This trick can sometimes be the answer when the dry fly on the surface isn't doing the job.

While traditional types of dry fly presentation will also work with smallmouths, the above techniques may help you when traditional techniques don't seem to be working.

Sub-Surface

Of the three sub-surface flies that were described in the chapter on fly patterns, the *"B" Damsel* is the only one that uses the lift and drop retrieve (or drift).

What is the lift and drop drift? Have you ever noticed when you are fishing a nymph or streamer that your strike comes at the end of the swing? Have you ever wondered how and why they hit at this point?

My theory is that predatory fish in a river or stream are generally looking upstream for their next meal; food flows down to them. As a minnow or nymph is dislodged from its holding area, the current will push the insect or minnow downstream. A minnow, to control its swimming, needs to go faster or slower than the current. As it approaches the predator, it tries to swim away from the imminent danger, but the current is still pushing its tail. The minnow, in its plight, will head to the side of the feeding fish, causing it to swim in a curved swing. This is the exact swing that your fly line makes at the end of your cast. A minnow or insect does not attack a predator. The evasive movement is a natural scenario for fish that are feeding, and is the trigger that causes the fish to strike; they think the food is getting away.

With the nymph, this pattern works for two reasons: First, the nymph has the same problem that the minnow has — current pushing it. It also sees the fish, but certainly at a much closer range. Its instinct is still to get away, causing the same curved swimming pattern. Second, nymphs also rise to the surface to emerge from the water to hatch. This is another trigger for the feeding fish.

In both scenarios the predatory fish is accustomed to the food reacting in the same way. Why not make this natural movement happen again and again on your cast?

This is easily accomplished by using the 5-foot sink-tip that

Smaller rivers can hold some nice smallmouth.

we discussed in the chapter on equipment and lines. This line will offer the control to allow the technique to work time and again.

By lifting and slowly lowering the rod tip during the drift downstream, you will duplicate the same movement that occurs at the end of the drift, but you will do it many times on the same drift, improving your chances of a strike each time that you lift the rod.

The most important aspect is to watch the rod tip and line where it enters the water. What does this mean? The area that I'm referring to is the point from the tip top of the rod to the point where the line first hits the water away from the tip. I call this section of the fly line the "loop." Most trout fishermen are taught to look at the junction of the fly line and the leader. This works well for dry flies, but won't work well for sinking or sink-tip lines. By concentrating on the loop at the rod tip, you will start seeing a uniformity to it, and will be able to see the subtle changes that occur from a strike. It is most important to see the strike; if you

like to look at the birds and trees, stop fishing and by all means look at them. But if you want to catch fish, watch the loop. Remember the strike tends to be subtle; any change in this loop can only be two things: the bottom or a fish's lips. Hopefully it is the latter, but admittedly I've stung many a rock in my life. Set the hook on anything that disrupts the normal loop.

I vary the rod lift from as little as a inch or two to as much as three feet. The longer lift will impart a greater movement to the fly and usually will take the more aggressive fish. The slight movement will cause the fly to stay closer to the bottom and will pick up

the less aggressive fish.

Remember that this lift and drop in conjunction with the checkerboard casting pattern will allow you to cover the water with overlapping casts and thoroughly fish the area.

Always impart a little movement to your flies; they are supposed to look alive, and you must make them do it. I almost never totally dead drift a fly.

Back to the sub-surface flies. The *"B" Damsel* will be fished as described above, but *Lefty's Red & White* and *Zonkers* are fished across the current with faster and longer strips. These two flies are my searching patterns. They cover a lot of water and help locate holding areas that the fish are using that day. These are also the flies used when fishing below a ledge or in the rapids. Here is where the most aggressive fish wait looking for a meal. These two flies will bring such fish up. Since the flies are only under the water a few inches, the strike is much like a surface strike. Generally, you will see the take.

Bottom-Bouncing

Fishing at or near the bottom should be your bread and butter fishing. This is where the fish feed and stay 95 percent of their lives, and this is where your best catches will come from.

The lift and drop retrieve and the overlapping casting pattern discussed previously will bring results. Watch your loop and you will catch fish.

All the bottom-bouncing patterns that were discussed in the fly chapter use the same lift. The *Clouser Minnow* can also be fished with long strips, generally across current. The strip can be 6 inches to as much as 3 feet long. Strip it fast or with a pause during the strip; the fish will tell you when you get it right. Experiment with different retrieves; on any given day one will work better than another. Accomplishing the longer strip with the Clouser requires you to stand a little diagonally to the current to allow your stripping hand to slide past your side. This strip was named the "Susquehanna River Strip" by Bob Clouser. The fish will jump all over this retrieve at times.

Fish can be both above and below the ledge, at different times.

Chapter 5

THE SEASONS

Let's look at the seasons in more detail. Though the exact times of the seasonal changes will vary from area to area, there will be consistent patterns that the smallmouth will follow no matter where you are.

Winter

Winter smallmouthing in my area mostly confines you to the few warm-water power plant discharge facilities on the Potomac River. These discharge areas typically warm the water comfortably above the rest of the river. There is also one on the Susquehanna at York Haven. Check with your local fly shop for other winter haunts.

Power plant discharges can provide great winter fishing.

If you are looking for the biggest smallmouth of the year, winter fishing can provide this. It's a different type of fishing, and you may get only one fish a day. I'm not personally fond of fishing this way, but if you are, I'll try to explain where these big-fish areas are, and they aren't at the warm-water discharges.

They are along the shore where the current flows past a sand or gravel bar. The water needs to be four feet deep or more. The largest of the smallmouth bass will come here to look for a meal during the winter months. Remember, fish are cold blooded and their metabolism is operating at a slow pace, so they don't require a large amount of food per day. As a matter of fact, they may only feed once or twice a week, and for a very short time. This is slow fishing, with sinking lines and minnow or crawfish imitations on the bottom. Casts to the same area using the same drift will have to be repeated over and over to get a strike.

Cast upstream and allow the fly to sink near the bottom and follow the drift down with the rod tip held high, much like you would do drifting a nymph down current for trout. Patience is the word here.

A good sign. . . the power plant is operating.

I like my winter fishing to be a little faster, so I look to the discharges. Federal regulations require these facilities to keep no more than a twenty degree differential from river water entering the plant to water being discharged from the plant. In January, the Potomac River's water temperature will run from 32 to 38 degrees, so the discharge water can be from 52 to 58 degrees. Such temperatures are warm enough to keep the fish pretty active during the day. You can keep "gentleman's hours;" the best fishing will be from ten in the morning until about three in the afternoon, the warmest part of the day.

I tend to fish weighted brown or black *wooly buggers* in sizes 6 to 12. Also in January, there will be a black stone fly hatch sometime mid-month into the second week of February. When the fish are taking these flies on the surface, a small size 16 or 18 brown or black elk hair caddis will bring strikes. I have fished these flies in a snow storm and caught fish. I remember a time we were fishing one midmorning with the air temperature at 13 degrees, and we were still taking fish on the surface. If you need relief from "cabin fever," this can be your answer.

The best times in your area, of course, might vary. Check with the shops and remember this is winter, wear warm clothes, a warm hat and neoprene waders. Keeping your hands warm is nearly impossible, but I find that finger-less gloves help a lot.

Spring

Mid-April to mid-June will find the fish in back-eddies near the shore or in eddies behind structure. This dead water is attractive to fish because they can expend very little energy while waiting for a meal. The baitfish will also be in the same areas.

Crystal buggers, *wooly buggers* and *Clouser Minnows* with a sink-tip line are the ticket. Make your cast close to you and at the tail of the eddy. Work your way up the eddy to the structure. This way any fish you hook will run out to the deeper water and your chances of catching numerous fish from one eddy are increased. I once caught 31 smallmouth up to 16 inches long from one large eddy below a group of rocks on the first of May. Again,

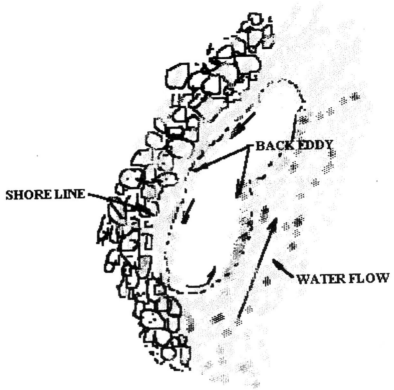

This is one of the best areas to find large smallmouths in the colder months.

fish the area thoroughly.

Shore line eddies also are effective at this time; just wade out till you're twenty to thirty feet from the bank and make your cast drift close to shore with the swing coming away from the bank and below you. Crystal Buggers and wooly buggers are my choice. Just keep moving downstream and repeatedly cast so that your casts will overlap on the swing. Bass will be along the shore looking for minnows. At times, they may only be in a few inches of

water. I have had great days fishing this way, while the boat fisherman I talked to at the ramps said that the fishing was slow. Remember, the water is still in the mid-fifties or a little higher, and the fish want their food with a minimum of energy expended. They aren't out in the middle of the river fighting the current, they are in the still water.

Summer

From June to October the fish are at their most active. Top water poppers and dry flies will be effective, as well as all of the sub-surface and bottom bouncing flies. Try different flies and retrieves until you find a pattern that works.

Fish above and below any ledges. During spring and early summer, the water below the ledge will be the most productive. As the summer wears on, the front of the ledge is the place to fish. This is where the larger fish wait for their food. The biggest fish will take the first seat at the dining room in the back-eddies above the ledge.

Fall

October is one of the best months in Maryland waters, and in many other places as well. This is the time for the fish to put on their winter fat, so they often feed all day, if the water is warm enough. This is great surface fishing time, even if you don't see any surface activity. Fish can usually be called up to a popper because they are most aggressive at this time of year.

In some years, early November can be like October, but soon the fish will start to retreat to their winter homes. There they will wait out the cold until that first warm day in Spring rouses them for another fishing season.

Conclusion

I hope the information presented will help you to improve your fishing experience, but remember, there is no substitute for time on the water. The more you can get out and fish, the more insight you will absorb about what the fish do at different times and under different conditions. I'm sure we all agree that no two fishing expeditions are ever the same. It's one of the great attractions of the sport. Nevertheless, the more you can go fishing, trying the various flies and techniques discussed in this book, the more successful you will be.

Good luck and good fishing!